# Sandyford & Cradlewell



by

Alan Morgan

Published by

Newcastle Libraries
& Information Service

Acknowledgments:

Many thanks are due to Jimmy Donald, who has a vast knowledge of this part of the world, and to Brian Bennison for his helpful information on the public houses of the area.

Photographic acknowledgments:

All photographs are copyright of Newcastle Libraries & Information Service except for the following:
5: Roger Fern;
14, 18: City Repro;
20: Ward Philipson Group Ltd.

ISBN: 1 85795 089 5



City of Newcastle upon Tyne,
Education & Libraries Directorate,
Newcastle Libraries & Information Service,
1998

Front cover:

In 1759 Cuthbert Lambert of H.M. Customs and son of a well-known Newcastle physician, Dr Lambert of Pilgrim Street was riding his horse along Sandyford Lane when it took fright and bolted ahead towards Benton Lane. Unable to negotiate the awkward left turn across Sandyford Bridge (over the Sandyford Burn) the frightened mare continued straight ahead, jumped the bridge parapet, and into the ravine below 'making a leap of forty-five feet and thirty-six perpendicular'. Lambert was lucky enough to cling on to the branch of an ash tree and apart from shock suffered no serious injuries. The heavier horse, however, plunged to its death with every joint said to have been dislocated.

Twelve years later a repeat accident occurred when a servant of Sir John Hussey Delaval survived only to find his seriously injured horse at the foot of the ravine. The horse had to be shot.

Again in 1827 a young Newcastle surgeon, John Nicholson, was not so fortunate at this accident black spot. This time the rider was killed and the horse survived. Whilst jumping the parapet the original incised coping stone commemorating Lambert's Leap of 1759 was dislodged, fell into the ravine and needed replacement.

For your information …

Copies of photographs which are copyright of Newcastle Libraries & Information Service may be ordered and purchased from the Local Studies Section, Newcastle City Library.

Also by Alan Morgan:
*Bygone Shieldfield,*
*Bygone Lower Ouseburn,*
*Bygone Jesmond Vale*
£1.95 each.

City Tours visit the City and suburbs during the Summer months. A free brochure is available from the City and Tourist Information Service, Newcastle City Library.

A free brochure detailing other local history publications is also available from Newcastle City Library.

For information on any of the above contact

Publications
City Library
Princess Square
Newcastle upon Tyne
NE99 1DX

or telephone 0191 261 0691 ext. 232.

**The extent of Sandyford and Cradlewell as defined by this book may be seen from the map on page 5. The area was probably as popular in prehistoric times as today, and two important relics have been found locally which date back around 4,000 years to the Bronze Age.**

Much of Sandyford and all of Cradlewell originally lay within the Township of Jesmond which was more extensive than Jesmond is today, reaching down to the Tyne where a salmon fishery is thought to have existed. In 1835 the Township of Jesmond was incorporated into Newcastle town.

Some buildings in the Cradlewell area have carried the name 'Minories' at one time or another. A Minories Farm, at the junction of what is now Sandyford Road and Jesmond Road appears on an 1830s map. The premises were reconstructed in 1857 and are now occupied by a firm specialising in 'architectural reclamation services'. Part of the earlier farm complex became the Punch Bowl pub, though it was rebuilt in the Scottish Baronial style in the 1870s. The Minories Farm land extended as far west as Brandling Place.

Minories was the name of the first English monastery of Franciscan nuns (Poor Clares, also known as Minoresses) which was established in 1293 in London. Apparently the Order never reached Newcastle so it remains a mystery as to why and when the area at the edge of Cradlewell assumed the name of Minories though it is worth remembering that the district had strong religious connections. The Franciscans were based near the Pilgrim Gate of the Town Wall (just off the present day Pilgrim Street), and with St Mary's Chapel and a Holy Well in Jesmond where miracles were said to have occurred, it may be that a hospice for pilgrims was located at or near the Minories Farm.

During the 14th and 15th centuries there are references to a windmill thought to have been situated on a site near to what became Sandyford School on Starbeck Avenue and Mill Lane (now Goldspink Lane). Mill Lane may have acquired its name, however, because it was the access road to the watermill in Jesmond Vale.

The owner of Sandyford Stone (the site of the eventual brewery) is mentioned among the Jesmond voters in the election of 1710, signifying a freeholder with land worth more than £10 per annum. In 1739 a Ralph Naters is on record as moving into a 'messuage' or cottage adjacent to Mill Close (and the windmill). In 1801 Baillie wrote in his 'Impartial History of Newcastle': 'In the vicinity of Newcastle, at Sandiford is a very large brewery, and of long standing, the property of Mr Naiters'. He goes on to describe it as one of the 'most respectable' of the numerous breweries in the town. Clearly Naters subsequently developed the site considerably.

Sandyford House, Naters' residence, appears to have been the earliest of the seven mansions built in the area and probably was erected simultaneously with the brewery close to the banks of the Sandyford Burn that fed into the Ouseburn via Sandyford Dean (otherwise known as Dropping Well Ravine or Rosedale). Sandyford House was rebuilt in the early 19th century. The open land to the east of Sandyford House, mainly in the Cradlewell area, was later occupied by six other mansions, each standing in their own grounds. Before 1818 Jesmond Park was built for Armorer Donkin and Goldspink Hall for Robert Clayton. In 1817 Villa Real was created for Captain John Dutton. In 1856 57 Broomfield Tower (renamed Minories) was constructed for Edward Nathaniel Grace. In the 1860s South Minories (confusingly renamed Broomfield Hall) was erected and during the 1880s Clement Stephenson became the first occupant of Sandyford Villa.

The beginnings of more general housing developments began around the early 1820s near Barras Bridge with Lovaine Row and Lovaine Place being the first streets to be completed. In 1827, Eneas

Mackenzie in his 'History of Newcastle' refers to them as 'a handsome range of houses' with Lovaine Row 'commanding a view of the north part of Percy Street and the Magdalene Field'. Lovaine Place which stretched eastwards from Lovaine Row deserved even more praise: 'it possesses the advantage of a fine, open, southern aspect, and of an interesting view down Pandon Dean and the River Tyne with each house having a large plot of garden-ground in front (down to the Pandon Burn) and ample space for convenient offices behind. It is one of the sweetest situations in the vicinity of the town'. Typical occupants at that time included a solicitor, insurance broker, an army colonel, and 'gentlemen', one of whom, a Joseph Nixon, owned most of the surrounding land and subsequently sold most of it for building sites.

During the 1840s and 1850s as the Pandon Burn began to be infilled (initially with soil coming from the newly excavated and nearby Victoria Tunnel) the housing development spread in an easterly direction along Sandyford Lane: Nixon Street (1844), Lovaine Terrace (1844), Simpson Street (1850), Lovaine Crescent (1850) around the perimeter of Pandon Dean; York Street (1853) later renamed Hood Street and then Race Street , Day Street (1855) and finally Alma Street and Marianople Street (1857).

By the 1860s Sandyford Lane appears to have been largely built as far as the Sandyford Burn (Lambert's Leap) except for the land adjoining the proposed railway development. The Blyth and Tyne Railway opened their new line from the New Bridge Street terminus to the Coast in 1864 and shortly afterwards adjacent housing developments were completed.

In 1878 Sandyford Lane was renamed Sandyford Road and a few years after was extended east of Lambert's Leap to include what had previously been known as Benton lane as far as the junction with Jesmond Road.

Pressure arose for more general housing about 1890 and it was agreed that, when the opportunity arose, some of the mansions and their extensive grounds east of Sandyford Dean would be acquired for residential development. The first property to come on to the market was the Sandyford Estate in 1892 following the death of the brewer J.S. Arnison. Sandyford House was demolished, the Sandyford Burn infilled and housing sprang up around the brewery site and as far east as Goldspink Lane during 1896-98. In 1899 the Goldspink Hall Estate was sold and the ten-acre site between Goldspink Lane and Villa Real was covered with new housing. Finally, following the death of R.G. Hoare at Jesmond Park, also in 1899, land at the north end of Cradlewell was developed during the period 1904-7 with streets named after British Cabinet Ministers.

The major redevelopment and motorway construction of the 1960s focussed on that stretch of Sandyford between Barras Bridge and the railway primarily to make way for a new Civic Centre, part of the motorway, and educational buildings that eventually became the University of Northumbria. Streets from Lovaine Row to Marianople Street were systematically demolished and Sandyford Road realigned.

Ten years later the proposed Cradlewell bypass scheme, ultimately aborted, necessitated the removal of three more of the 19th century mansions: St Catherine's Convent (Minories), formerly Broomfield Tower; Broomfield Hall, formerly South Minories; and Sandyford Villa. Of the original seven stately homes only Villa Real remains (hidden from view by buildings and trees), and though a listed building, redevelopment of the surrounding area is taking place.

An interesting feature at the corner of Sandyford Road and Portland Road is a rare Edward VIII pillar box cast in 1936 during his brief reign of ten months.

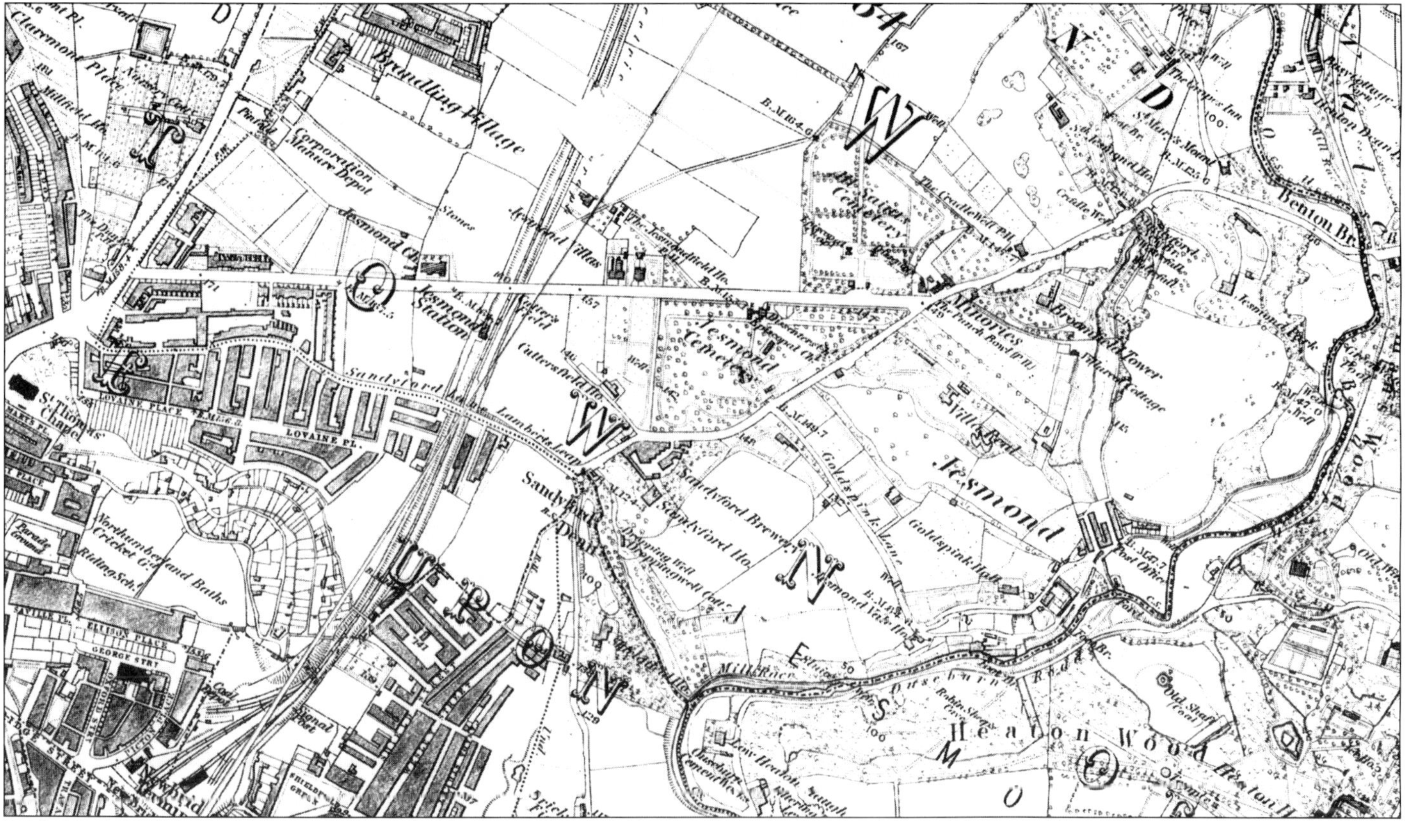


1. Sandyford and Cradlewell, for the purposes of this booklet, lie largely between Sandyford Lane / Benton Lane to the north, the Pandon Burn to the south and west, with the Ouseburn to the south and east. Benton Bridge (over the Ouseburn) is at the northern end while Barras Bridge (over the Pandon Burn) is at the southern extremity. The area is mostly on the higher ground above both streams even though the Sandyford across the Ouseburn is part of Jesmond Vale with a first reference date of 1384 (Sandeforthflat). This 1862 map shows Sandyford Dean roughly dividing the area in half. Lambert's Leap Bridge separates Sandyford Lane from Benton Lane. The railway is in course of construction (opening in 1864).

2. During the 19th century Cradle Well was a popular rural venue for publicans to obtain 'pure water to mix spirits with' and for the general public to 'drink fresh spring water'. Little did they realise that for many years the water had been supplied from reservoirs at Whittle Dean (near Horsley) because the earlier water supply had been ended by road widening. The original Cradle Well as shown in this drawing of 1894 consisted of three stone troughs in the shape of a cradle together with an iron ladle attached to the cradle head. It stood beside Benton Lane (now Jesmond Road) near where it crossed the Mill Burn (a tributary of the Ouseburn) at New Sandyford Bridge, almost at the site of today's replica at the foot of Osborne Avenue. New Sandyford Bridge was dangerous, with low parapets, and because it was feared that 'spirited horses might leap over', William Armstrong generously donated land for access improvements in about 1854. Nearly 50 years later, when the road was widened, the original Cradle Well was replaced with a 'substantial and well designed erection'. The ravine (Little Dene) leading to the Ouseburn was infilled, and the old stone troughs removed to Armstrong Park near King John's Well. The nearby Cradle Well public house as sketched above took its name from the water trough and first appeared in the directories of 1833. The present building was opened by Robert Deuchar in 1904.

3. Holy Trinity was one of two new churches in the area (the other being St Barnabas in Goldspink Lane) proposed around 1900 to cope with new residents. By the end of 1904 nearly £1,900 had been donated by the family of the late R.G. Hoare (the last resident of Jesmond Park upon whose land the church was to be built). The east end of the church was completed but insufficient funds delayed the project and a temporary iron church previously used on the St Barnabas site was transferred to accommodate the congregation. Consecrated in 1905, this 1912 photograph shows the temporary church at the west end of the chancel. The completion of the church (nave, tower and spire) began in 1920 and it was consecrated two years later as a War Memorial Church, largely financed by the family of R.S. Dalgliesh, a former Newcastle shipowner. The windows contain some fine stained glass showing badges of local regiments and stories commemorating the armed services. The weather vane is in the form of a ship.

4. This building was first of all Broomfield Tower, and later the Minories and stood in its own grounds opposite the Cradle Well pub. The spire of Holy Trinity is just visible. Broomfield Tower was built in the 1850s for Nathaniel Grace, a local land agent. By 1881 Arthur Coote, shipbuilder lived there with his wife, five children and seven servants. At this time the name was changed to 'Minories'. Alex Deuchar, wine and spirit merchant was the next occupant and after his death in 1913 it lay empty until St Catherine's Convent and Nursing Home moved there. At a later date a convent and preparatory school for boys were built in the grounds. The buildings were demolished in the late 1960s along with the nearby Broomfield Hall, in preparation for the ill fated bypass scheme, and a new convent and school built behind Nazareth House. The St Catherine's site is today occupied by the Leonard Cheshire Foundation and serves as a residential home, nursing home and day centre.

5. Villa Real, one of John Dobson's earliest designs, was built in 1817 for Captain John Dutton. Its original 21 acres of land included a fishpond and spring. This 1987 photograph shows the original fine Doric portico. In 1828, while occupied by Russell Blackbird a ship owner and insurance broker, Bronze Age relics were unearthed in the grounds. Subsequent occupants were William Wright (flint glass manufacturer) and Robert Harrison (tanner). In 1883 Dr Gribb, the surgeon of Blaydon Races fame, changed the name to Sandyford Park. After his death in 1916 the property was owned by the Poor Sisters of Nazareth for nearly 80 years, and known as Nazareth House. In 1996, the sisters transferred to London and for a while the house was managed by Catholic Care North East. They too have now moved on and at time of writing the building is up for sale.

6. A 1967 photograph of Sandyford House shortly before its demolition c.1970. It stood at the north end of Henderson Terrace, set back from Sandyford Road in part of the Villa Real estate, and appears to have been built in the early 1880s for Clement Stephenson, Chief Veterinary Inspector for Northumberland. In the 1920s the name was changed from Sandyford Villa to Sandyford House and in 1941 became home of the Roman Catholic Bishop of Hexham and Newcastle. In the 1950s it served as St Philomena's Hostel for working girls until its demise. The site is today occupied by retirement accommodation (Guardian Housing) known as Sandyford Park. The original gate pillars and wall remain standing.

7. In 1900, to cope with anticipated worshippers from the new housing developments, a temporary iron church was erected on a cramped corner on Springbank Road near the junction with Goldspink Lane. St Barnabas Church was completed nearly four years later a Chapel of Ease to Jesmond Parish Church. Parish Hall and vicarage followed, and the iron church was then moved to the Holy Trinity site. The church was demolished in 1977 and replaced by sheltered housing but the Church Hall was modernised to become a Church Centre, combining functions of church and church hall, for the joint parishes of St Barnabas and St Jude (Shieldfield), united in 1974. It was dedicated in 1978. The vicarage also survives. This c.1928 photograph shows the west side of St Barnabas with Helmsley Road to the left and Springbank Road to the right.

8. A 1948 photograph of Sandyford Road with an E class tram heading west towards the city. Fifty years later not a lot has changed except that buses have replaced trams and cobbles have been replaced with a more user-friendly surface. To the left Victoria Crescent (1896) is still in use (now largely student accommodation) and to the right the three-metre wall of Jesmond Old Cemetery (built in 1836 to deter grave robbers) is still intact though the stonework has deteriorated. Ahead the brewery buildings at the corner of Starbeck Avenue, owned by Robert Deuchar, have been converted into flats and offices which have entailed the renewal and replacement of some of the structures.

9. Sandyford School stood at the corner of Starbeck Avenue and Doncaster Road and was opened in 1898 to accommodate 1550 pupils (seniors, juniors and infants) in 22 classrooms at a cost of nearly £24,000. The site was originally part of the Sandyford Estate and a windmill stood here at least from the 14th century. This 1966 photograph shows the north side of the buildings with Robert Deuchar's brewery at far right and the caretaker's house to the left of centre. At times, before World War I, the school had to be closed for periods of up to three weeks to prevent the spread of contagious diseases. It was also closed when fumes from the nearby 'tip' became too unpleasant. Closing in 1984 it was demolished soon after and replaced by modern housing.

10. In 1801 the Sandyford Stone Brewery had long been standing in front of Sandyford House, home of Ralph Naters, overlooking Sandyford Dean through which a stream tumbled by way of Dropping Well to the Ouseburn. In 1812 quantities of worked stone chippings were found beneath the banks of the stream near Lambert's Leap. This may have been the site of the quarry for the original brewery, hence the name Sandyford Stone. Sandyford House was rebuilt in the 1820s by the Naters family to be followed some 20 years later by a redesigned brewery. In 1863 the business passed to Naters' son-in-law and in 1892 Robert Deuchar bought it. At that time Sandyford House was demolished and the stream infilled. Brewing ceased at Sandyford early in the 20th century and the premises became a bottling store, offices and bonded warehouse.

11. The foundation stones of St Andrew's Kirk, Church of Scotland, and its church hall were laid in February 1905, opening a few months later. The Church of Scotland in Newcastle dates back to the 18th century when Sandgate was 'the favourite resort of poor and industrious adventurers from Scotland'. Many became keelmen on the river. The congregation gradually migrated north from the riverside. This 1965 photograph shows the brick building at the corner of Sandyford Road and Grantham Road before the latter was sealed off. Because the church was built over the infilled Sandyford Burn (of Lambert's Leap fame) it appears slightly below ground level. Robert Deuchar's Brewery Office (1904) is just visible at left.

12. This early photograph shows the bridge over the Sandyford Burn with the brewery buildings to the left and Sandyford House to the right. Though difficult to see on this photograph, the replacement 'Lambert's Leap 1759' incised coping stone is built into the bridge parapet just in front of the lodge. Writing in 1887, a local historian records 'no more exists of the pleasant lane [now Portland Road] which led from Lambert's Leap, past Shieldfield House towards Stepney' … 'Doubtless the Drop Well Ravine … will soon be filled up and the bridge cleared away'. As predicted the ravine was infilled and the bridge removed and the only link with the past today is the replacement 'Lambert's Leap' coping stone by the present bus stop. Even the Lambert's Leap pub, once on Sandyford Road between Simpson St and Race St, closed in 1971.

13. Sandyford Salem Methodist Church c.1910 on the corner of Sandyford Road and Portland Road. Opened in 1907 it was part of a church extension scheme replacing the Methodist Chapel in Prudhoe St. Built on a bankside near the infilled Sandyford Burn the new church accommodated a large gymnasium and additional rooms under the church hall. Designed by W.H. Knowles a proposed 70ft tower never materialised. In the 1930s the gymnasium was used as a training school for the unemployed and in 1968 the site was cleared for Benton House. The ash tree in the photograph has been retained and incorporated into the pavement. Note the Brewery chimney and part of the Church of Scotland to the left.

14. Jesmond Station opened in 1864 as part of the Blyth and Tyne Railway Company's enterprising connection of Newcastle to the Coast and existing rail network in S.E. Northumberland. Coal could now reach Newcastle more efficiently, seaside traffic was lucrative, and the race goers to the racecourse on the nearby Town Moor could be provided with 'spacious and commodious platforms'. After 1864 building continued east along Sandyford Lane, and the stretch on the south side became known as North Carolina Terrace. In the late 1860s the Jesmond Station Hotel was opened at no. 12. James Deuchar became innkeeper c.1875. The premises were extended in 1938 but closed 32 years later. This 1971 view shows the Hotel next to the bridge just before demolition. The site of the hotel is adjacent to the present T.A. Centre. The station itself has now closed.

15. A 1971 view towards the corner of Sandyford Road and Marianople St immediately before demolition. The photographer is at the junction of Sandyford Road and Archbold Terrace. James Archbold owned much land in southern Jesmond and was Mayor in 1846. Forster's general store, together with the Post Office next door, were built in the early 1860s and for many years the corner site was occupied by T. Leathard, grocer and beer retailer, before moving next to Harrison Place. To the left of Spedding's shop (newsagent and tobacconist) was North Carolina Terrace that stretched a short distance to the Jesmond Station Hotel. In the background can be seen two of the modern buildings now part of the University of Northumbria. The tall building is Claude Gibb Hall (one time Chairman and M.D. of C.A. Parsons & Co. Ltd) with Ellison building at left.

16. Sandyford Academy, one of many educational establishments in the town, stood at the corner of Sandyford Road and Nixon St and began to operate as a boys' school in 1869. The house dates from the 1840s. This early 1890s photograph shows the Nixon St entrance. The founder, Robert Wilson who continued as Principal until 1919, gave his pupils 'a thoroughly practical education' rather than wasting time on 'totally useless' subjects. The school prepared candidates for Professional Preliminary Examinations, including medicine, and claimed a highly successful pass rate for a 'very short course of study'. The school continued until the mid-1950s when the building was taken over by the Northumberland and Durham Adoption Society. It was demolished in the early 1960s and the site lies partially under the University of Northumbria.

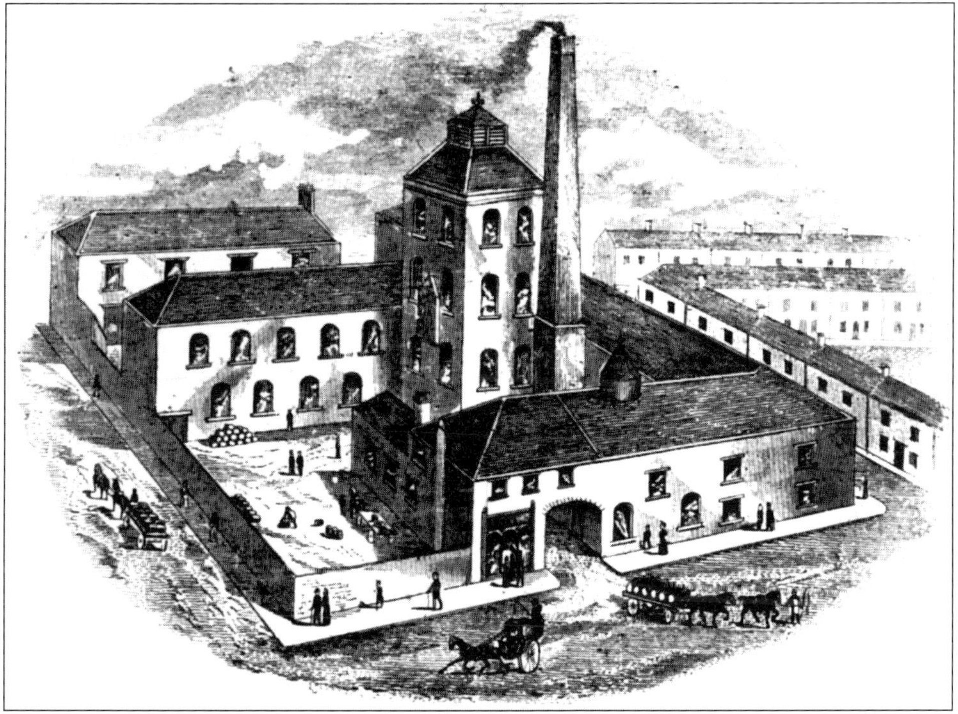

17. The Burton Brewery on Sandyford Road, and very close to Barras Bridge, was purpose-built for Robert Emmerson in 1880 on a site previously occupied by the Barras Bridge Malt Kilns which had belonged to Addison Potter of Heaton Hall. The drawing made c.1894 shows its frontage onto Sandyford Road. The brewery contained the latest technology including a powerful steam engine. Apart from the lofty tower and chimney stack other buildings comprised a laboratory, cooperage, stables, wine and spirits store, cigar store, offices and to the right of the entrance arch is a mineral water plant with ginger beer a speciality. An average of 100 barrels of beer and many thousands of bottles of aerated water were produced daily. Surrounding the brewery were streets of houses and shops which became known as Sandyford Square. On the opposite side of Sandyford Road was Sopwith's joinery works. Beer production appears to have ceased in 1907 and from then until the 1960s when demolition occurred, other businesses, particularly in the motor trade, took over. Today the area lies mainly under the realigned and much wider Sandyford Road between the Civic Centre and the University of Northumbria.

18. A 1967 photograph taken from the corner of Sandyford Road and Race St towards some typical two-storey terrace 1840s housing. The end shop window had been the premises of a beer retailer. The tall building behind is the west side of Victoria Square which contained substantial and prestigious three-storey dwellings (plus basements) inhabited by mainly business and professional families. The west side of the Square was known originally as Victoria Terrace (1845-6) and the east side as Albert Terrace (1868-9) with gardens in between. In 1873-4 both terraces merged to form Victoria Square. Only Victoria Square West has survived the massive redevelopment of the late 1960s. The Dene Motor Co. began as bicycle manufacturers at Haymarket around 1906. They progressed to motor cycles and finally to motor cars from around 1925, both here and at Haymarket.

19. Lovaine Place c.1957 from the gardens opposite which originally sloped down to the Pandon Burn. These substantial houses were built in the early 1820s and occupants included an army colonel, ship's captain, and a ship and insurance broker. Note the decorative balconies which escaped the recycling drive of World War Two because of their function in the prevention of accidents. Before infilling of the Pandon Burn in the mid-19th century these houses had an open view down Pandon Dean to the Tyne – 'one of the sweetest situations in the vicinity of the town'. 'Lovaine' appears to be derived from Louvain and has connections with the Northumbrian Percy family. Further along the street was the Lovaine Hall used by the German Lutherans as their place of worship from 1908 to 1963. Today the area is entirely covered by the Civic Centre.

20. Barras Bridge is at lower left in this 1958 view. Jesmond Road leads away to the Cemeteries and Cradlewell. Sandyford Road curves in the direction of the Sandyford Stone Brewery and beyond. At the extreme right St Mary's Place stretches towards Lovaine Crescent. Lovaine Row is lower centre with Lovaine Place at right angles. On the left side of Sandyford Road is the Drill Hall, Cabinet Factory, Saw Mills, Victoria Square and Archbold Terrace. On the right side we can see Newcastle Ambulance Depot, site of the Burton Brewery, and the terraces of Nixon St, Simpson St, Race St, Day St, Alma St and Marianople St. Most of the area between Jesmond Road and St Mary's Place was redeveloped in the 1960s but a mature hawthorn tree that stood near the corner of Lovaine Terrace and Lovaine Crescent survives in the University of Northumbria quadrangle.